The pressure of all that light

The pressure of all that light

Holly Painter

REBEL SATORI PRESS

NEW ORLEANS

Published in the United States of America by
Rebel Satori Press
www.rebelsatoripress.com

Paperback ISBN: 978-1-60864-210-6
ebook ISBN: 978-1-60864-223-6
Library of Congress Control Number: 2022942249

For Emily Beam, my throughline and my love

Contents

Michigan

Auto Pilot

Instrument panel / Lite Brite code

Wild blue yonder / dead end road

Biplane wings / ear fuzz flaps

Ejection seat / my mama's lap

Peaches

Mom? What's a sex change?

The wooden spoon slows in the pot.
Hissing flecks of tomato soup
fling themselves at my mother's hand.

Where did you hear that?

I'm returning from the pantry with peaches,
sunshine slices floating in a sea of syrup
inside the aluminum can.

At camp. Some kids said I should get a sex change.

My mother twists a knob beside the burner.
The glowing spiral fades quickly to gray
and appears cool.

A sex change is when a man becomes a woman. Or vice-versa.

I pick at the peach can label
with a close-bitten thumbnail.
The edge accordions, stuck fast with a strip of glue.

How?

My mother takes the can from me and slides a knife
cleanly under the label, adding it to the pile
she'll mail in to support my school.

They have surgery. Sometimes lots of surgeries.

I drag my stool over to the can opener
and let the magnet grab the can then spin it,
wobbling like a warped record.

Can kids do it?

She shoots out a hand to grab the can
as the top lifts off, a jaggedy-brimmed hat
I shouldn't touch.

No. And don't listen to those kids at camp.
Just because you like Legos and sports doesn't
make you a boy. Now go tell Dad it's dinnertime.

She flips the peaches into a bowl and turns
to check on the chicken in the oven.
I nod okay. Okay. I'm okay. I'm okay.

The Strait

There is no street where I live.
The leaves of houseplants rattle.
Scorched earth and fire escapes,
the city beside the strait.

Only the inner layers pasted over remain.
Today is not a shade of anything:
a city grown tired of rebirth,
of the scent of raspberries and wood.

The place that made our cars
will open itself to me tonight
on land that cannot be new
as the hush or the day or

the air blowing cold
between rotting boards.
The scaffolding of a rust empire
with wild dogs for sentries.

Shedd Aquarium

Inside is marble-bricked white,
walls like an igloo and I wonder
if my tongue would freeze.

The seahorses are wrong:
spiny, Trojan armor-plated,
their tails on backwards like g's,
not the wise little q's I imagined.

Lungfish are huge Petoskey stone poos
dropped in dull water. A sign says
their appearance is camouflage
but the other kids point – *Ewww!*

It's only disguise. I know.
Their fears are bigger than this.

Assembly

Who knows how to do a push-up?
I need volunteers!

Jumping Jack jogs around the stage as he talks.
An orange sweatband restrains frizzy curls
as a matching stopwatch bounces on his chest.
Exercise is his *thing*.

At 7, I'm all kid muscle: rangy and wound-up.
I love Little League. I love pick-up soccer.
I love the Presidential Physical Fitness Test
badges my mom's sewn onto my jean jacket.

I love these assemblies.

Ben and I grin at each other as we climb the steps.

Now boys' bodies and girls' bodies
are a little bit different, aren't they?

PENIS! comes a shout from the back.
Jumping Jack misses a jog.
A teacher hisses, deploying
cross eyebrows and a warning finger.

For boys' bodies, this is the right kind of push-up.

Jumping Jack drops to the stage and performs
a basic push-up, the kind we do in gym class.
Ben and I scramble into position, poised to dip,
but Jumping Jack catches my arm and pulls me up.

But girls have less upper-body strength,
so put your knees on the floor instead.

He demonstrates a clearly wimpier push-up.
Ben is pumping up and down, eyes on the floor.
No! I shout as Jumping Jack poses my limbs.
He flinches. The room goes quiet. My eyes burn.

I don't need a girl way! I can do it right!

The principal takes my hand and walks me offstage.
Jumping Jack gets another volunteer.

Eight

Clouds dangle over telephone lines,
fingertips poised to pluck a guitar.

Ben hangs upside-down from the tire swing
jabbing at roly-polies until his stick snaps.

He dismounts with a neat somersault and
brushes the woodchips from his ecto green windbreaker.

Next year, his parents will split. He'll move with his mom
to the neighborhood where the wild boys live.

I climb the slide, boots slip-squeaking,
and thump up to a landing caked with wet-pulped leaves.

He'll take pills in high school and get suspended for fighting.
I'll rack up scholarships and slice myself with broken lightbulbs.

Wanna come over to my house?
I'll race you!

I scan the woods where we're not allowed to go.
It's almost dark, there are no birds, and we run.

Lone Pine Cemetery

Rain between the digging
and the burying means
summer afternoons of
muddy swimming holes.

We leap from earthmovers,
shrieking as we plunge underground,
balloon our breath in our cheeks,
and spit out dirty bubbles.

We slice a worm with a spade
and the dead fall out
but we are small gods:
we've made another worm.

We dart between stones.
Beloved wives provide cover
as we hide from each other,
shivering.

We sprawl in new grass
thin tufts in the soil,
look straight up the rain
to the black

and try to imagine
dirt coming down,
holding us underground,
silent and still.

Please don't hurt me

The first time I'm attacked in a bathroom,
I'm six, ketchup-smeared, wild. An elderly woman
swings her Mary Poppins bag at my tiny body.
Get outta here, you nasty little boy!
Slip on the tile, bang my knee, but no blood,
so I run off to find my mom.

I don't always tell Mom.
I'm eleven: a guard, summoned by a bathroom
cleaner, arrives armed with a bludgeon.
Hands up, dripping, I plead with the woman:
You can check if you want! I'm not a boy!
She wrestles me to the ground, pats down my body.

Short hair; sturdy gait; lean, muscular body.
Dresses; headbands; sparkly earrings – my mom
wants the world to know I'm not a boy.
But in the YMCA locker room, the mall bathroom,
there's a posse of preteens, a clumpy-lashed woman
at the mirror. *The fuck are you doing here?* Blood-

curdling scream, keys turned claws, drawing blood.
Outside, a boyfriend, a husband, somebody's
dad. *Just saw some perv sneak into the women's
room!* They wait, nails biting palms. If Mom's
not there to diffuse when I leave the bathroom,
then I have to be ready to run, faster than those boys,

those men. But they're not wrong: I am a boy,
or I would be. The day I start to bleed,
week shy of my twelfth birthday, I cry in the bathroom.
Pink day-of-the-week undies soaked red, body
unrecognizable, a traitor. I don't tell my mom.
I don't want to become a woman.

What's wrong with being a woman?
Back-to-school shopping at Target, boys'
section, me begging, *Please? But Ryan's mom
lets him wear baggy jeans!* Under a blood-
red bullseye, she breaks down. Sobs shake her body.
What's so awful about being like me? In the bathroom,

she fixes her makeup, feels the women notice her blood-
shot eyes. I wait in boys' apparel, curse my stupid body
and myself for making Mom cry in the Target bathroom.

Field Trip

Bus windows stutter open.
Calves & thighs adhere to grey institutional vinyl.

Squeals bounce

      Dawson's Creek &

Jay-Z

      &

            who's asked which U of D boy to prom.

Our teacher stands, grabs hold of a seat
as we lurch through the parking lot:

      Girls! Girls! Quiet down!

That lasts two minutes. My plaid-skirted classmates
are back onto *Gilmore Girls*, AP bio, field hockey.

            Beside me, my best friend.

I haven't slept well since we met a year ago.
My math notebook curls with letters I can't give her

& my wallet holds as treasure the one she wrote me

mundane but signed *love*

as all these girls sign notes, link arms in the halls,
hang photos of friends in lockers, braid hair in class

so casual in their intimacies

while I cry in the library at lunch, headphones on:

*ohhh oh, you're too afraid to touch
too afraid you'll like it too much*

My crush, my love, my all-consuming shame & hunger

for whom I regularly lie & make excuses
whom I enable & save & spend quarter after quarter
talking down from pay phones around town

asks me what I'm reading.

In my lap, a library book: *Slaughterhouse-Five.*

She smiles, *So it goes.*

My chest clenches.

I turn my pages, try to breathe normally

not be aware of her clinking rings

her laundry soap that's different from mine

her bare banged-up knees tucked neatly under the seat

smoothness grazing my legs at every thumping turn.

Billy was helped to his feet by the lovely boy, by the heavenly androgyne.

I read the sentence three times before nudging her.

Do you know what this word means? Androgyne?

She smiles again, too slowly
finds my eyes &
holds my gaze too long.

Yeah. It's like you. Not quite a boy or a girl. Or hard to tell.

Two girls belt out Britney Spears.
Someone chews watermelon bubble gum.
The bus rumbles onto I-75.

The wind blows my first love's hair across her face &

I have flaming cheeks &
a word for myself.

Feed Me

Feed me only what is necessary.
What is tender might be necessary.

Feed me the chain of clay beads
encircling your wrist

boxcar brown, a burlap sack
caked with the mud of potatoes.

Feed me the red you suck off a candy cane
leaving a stabbing white icicle.

Then feed me the icicle
the seasonal stalactite

that drips itself to life and death
Melt it for me with your breath.

Feed me your grab bag face:
your punched in nose and

overplucked eyebrows,
never quite symmetrical.

Feed my teenage demand
that you be everything:

dinner, lunch, and breakfast
morning, noon, and night.

Feed me only what is necessary
and all you are is necessary.

Padiddle

noun

    *a driving game in which players spot cars with only one
headlight – in one variant, after a player calls a padiddle,
each other player must remove an article of clothing*

Dog Star brings rain, dousing syrup-dense summer
with sheets of relief, floating fishfly corpses into gutters.
We three mutineers board our homegrown hunk of metal
driver-side headlight past its finicky death throes.

Sweet summertime summertime we slap on ballcaps
and muscle along Jefferson looking for others like us:
eighties two-tones, lewd pirate-patch eyes,
half-fizzled-out machines that make us primitive.

Padiddle! ceiling thumps reveal tattoos, piercings,
nipples, sparse swirls of body hair, sunburns –
blushing back freckles run together like
cookie sheets of egg-runny dough plops.

Spinning downtown, we slide low in our seats,
kinetic creases streaming chloride heat, roll up windows,
scatter our polycotton wrappers in naughty laundry piles
while I zigzag until, *Shit shit shit! The tunnel!*

We've missed the last U.S. exit and we're sunk
into echoing fluorescence, silent river above.
I take the underwater mile slow, ignore the honking
as we stuff ourselves into sleeves of any kind.

When we emerge, it's Welcome to Canada and
this way for duty-free and have your documents out
but we're grinning and dumb and shamelessly young.
We don't even know where our shoes are.

They tell me I am wicked and I believe them

Beneath the canopy of bulbs over I-94
my shadow, penumbra of knotted curls,
rises again and again on the back of the driver's seat
as classic country wars with evangelist radio static.

She sleeps in the front. Crying, silent, I watch her
below the sightlines of her mother's rearview mirror
digging fingernail into forearm to focus the pain
as I plead with the thunderclap God of Mt. Sinai:

Let me not love her.

Chicago, a college tour of icicles, shared double bed,
hummingbirds penned between quilt squares.
Slumbering mid-sentence, she breathes whole notes.
I wait an hour then slip an arm around her waist, absolved by sleep.

But I am not sleeping.

I am teaching myself to leave the people I love.
I breathe in her conditioner that smells like crayons.
I unfold a map in my head, uncreasing it on the table.
Where will I go in this world with all its wetnesses in blue?

California

To San Francisco with Paul

We abandon our vertical seasalt Legoland in a honking, steaming, close-cuddling procession of backlit raindrops trickling down too few finite rivulets. Foot brake-bound, I jabber, Paul nods, flits to another station, trains his camera to the top of the Aon Center – zoom, scan, pull back, looking for jumpers. None today, but he keeps skimming, US Bank, Wells Fargo. No, it's 2003, and everyone's happy.

We lose our tagalong convoy within the hour and then there's just space and we can't figure out why LA's so crowded when here to San Francisco is just truck stops and oil derricks nodding and those crisp white wind turbines they thought would ruin the view but the view's just mountain crusts growing mold and creosote bushes stranded all across the flat like props from an earnest Western.

We're three weeks Californian and already possessive of our peeling paper trees, our envíos de dinero signs, our inland seagulls nibbling strip mall trash, three weeks friends and already possessive of the other's secret, packed tight and melancholy as the cows, scented miles away. Now we've said it, it's true, and we're going to San Francisco. In this state of strangers, there's no one to mind.

When the gutter-ball sun lands between rows of pistachio trees, we can only tell hills from sky because they're so much blacker and firmer than backcountry firmament with its pores to ease out the pressure of all that light. We'll arrive late to a scene that's all sparkle, hills and sky reversed. We'll find no underage bars in the Castro, so we'll eat Ben & Jerry's and watch our people and wonder what people we'll be.

But that's hours from now. We pull off for gas station tacos and sit in the forecourt dripping salsa and beans on our dusty flip flops. We have no people yet, Paul and me, just each other and the hope that there's no god to mind.

Apologetics of a College Freshman

To the termites of the last empire:
Sorry, but we chew our own now,
inflate our cities in the mornings
like sour apple bubblegum
and swallow them at night
not the other way around.

To the tobacconists of the old century:
Sorry, but we roll our own now,
stash Mom and Dad in the Christmas cupboard
and take them out to wrap around boxes,
crease their edges and trim the excess
while Mom's still flatly nattering away.

To the factory farmers of yesteryear:
Sorry, but we grow our own now,
sprinkle seeds in classroom plumbing,
children sprout from the walls,
absorb their math and science and then
we pluck them and send them to college in vases.

To the bankers of ages past:
Sorry, but we save our own now,
drop kisses in jam jars with buttons
and cursing coins and wishes and
every extra Sunday we save till the
end of our days and then spend.

To the gods of a time gone by:
Sorry, but we are our own now,
fathers, mothers, devils, angels
prophets, priests, chosen people
and if we seem a touch surreal
well, let's be honest, so were you.

Sonoran Song

Saguaro, gloating eight-headed phantom
of midnight coronations when the dust can't be seen.
Prickled crowns, no, blossoms so white they're invisible.

Kill the lights.
Don't forget how shy you were once.

Give me your hand.
A worried fingernail is the miner's pickaxe.
Crinkle a new mountain against the wind.

It's easy to remember when there's nothing to see
but fasten your eyes anyway.

What dry lonesome wind carries the desert's sermon?
Sand that never finds a home.

Listen, the coyote wails.
Will we all sing for our suppers?
Deluge my cupped palm beggar's bowl.

Quieter inside.
Thirsty whale ribs.
Swallow me.

Venice Beach

There's danish breakfast buffet for anyone who can amble past the Holiday Inn concierge like they have a right to be there in their bermuda shorts and tourist trap tees and a barefoot kwik-e mart with a sliding coldrush trunk of sticky-sleeve popsicles and everything else only two-deep shelved by the chemical-grime-punctured monarch of the checkout who'll sell beer for double food stamps but only between noon and one when his bicep-bloated boss sneaks two squirts each from the self-tan bottles in aisle three and swaggers out to Muscle Beach, that iron mesh fishbowl of drip-knotted chest hair and squiggle-veined grunting no-necks in sleek Speedos, breaking on benches beside the miniaturized tennis courts where gaggles of college girls smack their rackets in time with the elastic thump of Monday night drum circle with its droning hashish musk and four-hour dusk crescendo creeping under the catcalls of teenage taggers high on the Technicolor twists of their own names and taunting a pair of squatter guys, unwise to their belted smileys and pocketed fists clenching and unclenching like the Pacific, pulled up close to spit out some blond boys in midwinter wetsuits with their surfboards tucked underarm like the asymmetrical seagulls sifting through Styrofoam trash for scraps of carnival food discarded by boardwalkers gawking at a sword-swallowing skater or the scaly sand dragon re-sculpted daily with shovel and spoon by a bronze-tanned man who begins before the first podcast-strapped jogger, before the caricature artists arrive with their wobbly tabletop shops, before the beach police megaphone sounds its good morning and homeless kids wake between volleyball nets where the beach-sweeper doesn't go

The only shame

we drenched ourselves once in a field in Nebraska
pushed each other down in the rain, peeled our shirts
peeled our mouths from each other's nipples
that's two rings

they appreciate the symmetry
these strangers with their damp dollar bills

in those boots, you're six foot two
with a pierced-up face
bush shaved so they ache
for your sandpaper graze

cause now you've got yourself a smooth pole
slather it with sweat with spit
with any wet
they like it wet

mount it like the lamppost at Fourth and Main
where we played hacky-sack and
pretended not to notice each other
looking

the manager told you only topless
you told me only this once
and he lied and you lied and
now I'm parked outside

watching the night trains

engines welded cold to sirens
wishing myself into their carbon guts
to wake up charred and crisp and free
in any Mexico-town where you aren't

a plastic orchid, translucent
beside those neighborhood girls
I'm out of breath just sitting here
while you're in there and

the manager taps on my window:

You should love her better, he says

you cry because I cry but this is only
a lonely nighttime pickup game
a hot-lit hallucination and the only shame
is not loving you enough

The New Neighborhood

Chain link shadow cats, night cawing roosters,
pale mournful babies of quiet Latina ladies,
wild dogs dragging piñatas down sidewalks,
ghettobirds dip-diving, bellies full of cops.

Roadside fire sale: Happy Meal plastic gadgets,
Catholic school polo three cousins worn.
Bedsheets wreathed together by rain and dust.
Shopping cart, my own shopping cart, mine!

Mechanics' shoes scuff pews unstuffed on the
front lawn at Friendship Primitive Baptist Church.
An ice cream truck squeaks La Cucaracha and
it's *Tamale! Tamale! Tamale!* every morning.

Musica norteña wake up, mulitas on the breeze.
The blurry-dull sun leaks and you find
your Spanish dubbed out of sync like
everything else you think you remember.

The Man She Wants

His bookstore sells chapbooks.
Mine's about a woman who tried me for a year, left me for a man.

It happens a lot: straight woman, bi women, lesbians.
It's always a man that comes next.

What are you? he asks. *You look like a teenage boy.*
I leave my number to call if my books sell.

He calls the next day.
They haven't sold but do I want to go to the beach?

You thought I was a teenage boy.
But you're not. Besides, I like guys, too.

He kisses me at the beach, face big, stubbly, lips dry, tongue bloated.
I flinch, remember high school.

A week later, he invites me over.
Why are you doing this? Paul asks.

I want to know what's so great about men. What's better than me?
Men are shit, he says. *And this is a bad idea.*

I know. He hands me his car keys.
I have a car, but I might need an excuse to leave.
It's raining in Topanga Canyon.
I drive the car through a growing pond at a dip in the road.

He wants to have sex. I've had sex but not this kind.
I'm small, fingers numb, wrong kind of vulnerable.

I keep saying okay. Without enthusiasm, but okay.
We try. We can't. It hurts. He does it for himself while I wait.

He's made dinner: salad, ravioli, wine.
He's a good cook. He wants me to stay.

The sky grumbles. The windows are black.
I wonder about flooding on the road.

I'm still saying okay. We try again. We can't.
Paul calls. That's his job. I need to go. I need to go now.

The car makes it. I make it. I call my ex.
I shouldn't, but I want her to know

I'm making bad choices, punishing myself
for not being the man she wants.

Alternate Timeline

In God's preferred version
of this year's Christmas card
you're seven months pregnant
seven months on from our wedding.

I'm a man now, by the way,
with an untweezed moustache
and a paisley green cravat
that matches your maternity dress

at least in the sense that you're red
and I'm green and God may be
color-blind as a dog but He knows
the Christmas color grayscale tones

from watching *It's a Wonderful Life.*
We'll watch it too this year, in God's
preferred version of our Thanksgiving,
and not cringe at George Bailey's

tantrums but tear up at the final
family scene, and God will smile
when we don't pull out the tripod
for our yearly Christmas card picture
                              of two dykes and a dog.

The San Francisco Self-Examiner

Chomping heartburn pretzels, cruising high
over Santa Lucia's wrinkles, I'm scratching ballpoint
hearts, misshapen on elastic skin, through a hole
in my jeans. Nervous flier on this bounce to
LA, I lurch as the seatbelt light flicks on, but it's not clear
what's wrong. The sky's bottomless blue and there's nothing

out there but waves chewing the coast, a frothing
sheet of sea life, still and silent from this height.
Unsettled by my grave eyes and buzz cut in the clear
glass of the window, I try to look beyond to a point
outside but the Gestalt switch is flipped. I can't go back to
California seascape without seeing the whole

picture: the beautiful hunted look of androgyny, holed
up in a pressurized pocket of sky, foreground to that prettier thing –
relief at the end of a continent, that American edge I fled to
years ago, a sanctioned escape on cross-country highways,
shooting earnest self-portraits at every lookout point,
cultivating the uncertainty behind those clear

eager eyes. Now, in this rattling tube, even less is clear
than it was then. Children blink at me, and I tire of the whole
business of ambiguity: the gawking, the pointing,
the whispers, the strangers who need to know everything
about me. Enigmas are unwelcome on airplanes: I could be a hi-
jacker, a shoe-bomber, a lonely weirdo who's a little too

quiet. But who isn't lonely, who wanders in from the sea? To
go west we must first teeter east, circling until we're cleared
to rumble over the Inglewood grid and exchange weak high-
altitude air for a mantle of lethal yellow that makes the whole
city skyline seem antique, a sepia photograph, something
shown at LACMA centuries and civilizations on from its point

of origin. I close my eyes, and that startling moment, the point
when the ground is suddenly right there and wheels thump onto
the tarmac, jolts my stomach. Passengers collect their things
from overhead bins and Tetris them into the aisle. The cabin clears.
I slip from my seat like February's groundhog emerging from its hole,
spooked by its own shadow, by spectators scrutinizing from on high.

But such things are only ghosts, childhood echoes that sneer and point
as I step into the high smudged sun of this old desert, turning west to
breathe the sea air beneath the smog, an undercurrent clear and holy.

Save Our Souls

I have nothing but my hands
and this dark stuttering water,
an ocean of indifferent waves
lashing continents tied by their feet.

Needles drop into the sea,
the flat and raggedy blue
where a thousand cabin boys
have drowned in their hopes.

Cloudbreak sun, loose strand of light.
Go ahead. Blow out all your pink troubles,
your imperfect slabs of tenderness,
fuzzied with cold, and I'll wait.

When you tire of your homeland

Gather up one corner
and start walking away.

Stroll through a neighboring autumn.
Drag your native land over leaves
red and yellow like flattened peaches.

Stretch your home spaghetti-thin.
But careful! Not so fast!

When it becomes impractical
to tow your old life any farther
make your way to the national gallery.

There find the painting with a thousand snaking rivers
and thread your country up to the oily horizon.

New Zealand

Shipwrecked, I Arrive

body hair crusted in salt.

I put on the suit from the
government shipwreck kit
or the back rack of the
Dunedin hospice shop.

Dead man donor –
the hospital got his kidneys,
his liver, his heart.
I got his Sunday skin.

It's too big.
They expected me to be bigger
even after eight days on driftwood
knowing that Hell is blue.

I could be someone else here.
I could be someone else in this suit.
I'll call myself Holden.
Not the car – the liar.

But when it rains
the wet wool's a second drowning
so I walk into town naked and
everyone nods indulgently.

No one offers me clothes.
They assume this is my culture.

Dandelion

Asterisk-headed dandelion,
why no sleeping in the park?
Snoring spreads the seed, of course,
you whisper in the dark.

But what about, I ask you then,
The street-side row of lights?
It's them and not the sleepers
that go zzz all through the night.

The metal trees, you nod at me,
I guess they tend to drone.
They're talking to each other
while you just breathe alone.

I'm not alone! You're here with me!
But already, he slept silently

Her Blue Moons

She comes at last after months of drought,
of shepherd boys drinking the dew of the fields,
of zebras sharing the watering holes of lions.

She comes at last with the rains from the north,
flash floods, urchins who take to treetops like kites,
delicate monkeys who can neither swim nor drown.

She comes at last in the chill of an antique moon,
sallow, china blue hairline fractures around the eyes
and wrestles a pocket button for the last dry cigarette.

Her fingers scissor between mine.

The dance she drags
from our feet
one two three
one two three
one two threes us

past the glow of whitewashed warehouses
across the bridge where children watch cars
burn time-lapse streaks in the alleys,

beyond the sagging marquees
of an autumn fairground where silhouettes of
stiltmen gather fog in the clearing,

past the dairy and the post shop to a student flat,
three flatties, a woodstove, and David Attenborough
on the television telling us we're missing almost everything.

We Get On

like a house on fire. What a line. Nothing burns here.
My armpits grow mildew while I sleep and
stick insects weld watertight armor for storms.

Fistful of stars spattered at this latitude night after night
always the same, just tilted, and you picnic alone
on an island between eastbound and westbound.

I skid up close, toss tins of corn out the window.
Is this home? Where's your *God bless you*?
Take a photograph to hang in my kitchen. You cook.

Feed me oysters. I'm allergic to ragweed and shellfish
but what an aphrodisiac, to watch you shuck and pile
the soft parts in a shallow pool of vinegar.

I hold the door in spring. You press your nipples flat
against a sled on a dewy hill. It's faster than snow
and a salt truck sprays the ice-sculpted children.

I paint a pot of daffodils for your desk and put you to work
writing the story of my life, especially the part where
you sit on my bike and put your thumbs through the holes
                                        in my pockets.

Otago

If the Central Railway remained, we'd wheeze Vulcan diesel
236 kilometers past platforms sunk in gravel, procession of towns,
timing our thoughts to the clickety-clack.

Too late for railcars, we roam the motorways in an old station wagon,
windows down, our open hands gliding along the inland easterlies
as we trace Dr Frankenstein's mountainside sutures.

Through Milton and Balclutha, Roxburgh and Alex,
we travel a panorama that's always three-quarters sky
and the rest of it gorse spilling like mustard over every hill.

We picnic on blue cheese boulders in salads of scorched grass
and scrub homophobic scrawl from the Queenstown bungee bridges
that attract ambivalent suicides.

We hold strategy meetings in rickety gold shanties that pockmark
the Arrowtown ravines, fastening our maps flat and unscrolled
with century-old candleholders of crumbling green copper.

We watch ewes forage in the tussock, the searching shapes
a slightly lighter shade of lint, and in the distance, the Crown Ranges
pique a need for hot cinnamon buns smothered in fast melting sugar.

We're meant to flock to coasts, big cities with liberal leanings.
We're not expected to nest atop tire piles, to perform mating rituals
under the whispering trees, those naked bearded beggars.

But it happens here too, where the cold sun shines and
sea breezes never penetrate. In this ancestral anthill, amongst
a hundred muscular subterranean hearts, we find each other.

The day will be beautiful

My knuckles itch and I wonder if you've been tested lately,
if you parallel park correctly, in only three swipes,
if you would know how many times to thump my sternum
and how to seal my mouth with yours.

The day will be beautiful and it will be my duty to notice.

Your father posts us baggies of knotted walnuts
already freed from their shells.
We stay in bed all afternoon and don't go out
until the hailstones stop plopping on our roof.

The day is not beautiful but I don't notice.

At night, a toothpick alloy bridge straddles the tracks
and is oranger than anything else on the island.
We take pictures because we're together
while the streetlights jiggle like we can't keep still.

Comfortable Grunge

All of us are soft and easily bruised
flatulent boys of a kindlier youth
sleeping patterns of fur and dripping noses
careless rise and fall of mud-matted flanks

we'd bathe our lungs in comfortable grunge
wilting flower-weeds that miss the sun
yellowed upholstery with its own
nicotine cravings

on the radio
a recording of the tossing sea

imagine it
in the stately grey of old BBC broadcasts
wonder about waves you can't see

outside, the air is much too fine to breathe
donkeys chase nervous chickens
through the yard

Telephones

You   live in a Motown snowglobe
           a January whiteout
           a ballet of bobbing traffic lights.

I   have an unnatural summer birthday
           on an expanse of volcanic sand
           beside the Tasman Sea.

You   call early as the tuis one morning
           to ask if I'll stand up
           in your wedding.

I   have called you every week
           since I left Michigan
           and you did not.

You   offer up sharper details:
           he's afraid of daddy long legs
           and he smells like melted ice.

I   have new words that don't reach you:
           lollies and gumboots and one for the way
           the sun leaps up all at once, sheepish.

You   will be married on an island
           of forgotten fish bowls
           with wild deer for witnesses.

I   would wait in the woods in my red sea rig
           but red ribboned trees only worry about
           the tomorrow that cuts us off.

When you hear my voice but can't taste my breath
           it's not *death do us part*.
           It's just these telephones.

The way it felt to be so warm

I.

Three days and nights in the smoky gales of autumn
you stand there, one cracked leg wedged tight between posts.
Three days, but you only whimper, with meekest restraint:
Please Sir and *If you're not too busy* and *Is anyone at home?*

Three days, as you languish, an innocent shamed in the stocks,
we pace every last paddock, but when we finally find you,
you appear at first to be posing, a creature so eager to please that
you'd be poised on tiptoe for some pastoral portrait.

As we wrench free your fractured foot, you tremble,
a shivering core of wet-matted misery, moaning in protest
against the dew of the morning. With a panicked yelp,
you stumble, tumble, skid fast down the grass, thrashing,
crashing past the bent saplings, landing with a splash in the gully.

II.

and you remember the lights of the dancehall
on the beach of your Lake Michigan hometown;
and you remember dozing on the screened-in front porch
in the worm-scented rains of April;
and you remember sawdust on your boots
as your dad showed you how to use his handsaw;
and you remember your mother helping you
into your snowpants and coat and backpack;
and the way it felt to be so warm and bundled
made you sure you'd grow up to be an astronaut;
but now you realize you're just another sheep and you're dying.

III.

When we reach you in the ditch, you twitch at my touch
and someone sighs, *Curtains*, but I know your eyes are alive,
so four of us scrawny things wrap your battered frame in a blanket
and drag you back up the hill, filling our gumboots with mud.

At the doorstep, I wrest you from that sheet, carry you into bed,
and sink us both in its warmth as you nestle your head on my chest.
As I stroke the sodden tufts that mask a shattered skeleton,
you notice how my heartbeat changes whenever I swallow
but sleep comes to you before you can tell me.

Her Teeth

They're crooked. Not like the politicians my father harangued over Easter ham. More like the zigzag seawall on which I wobbled as a child, fingertips outstretched for balance, one hand over the thumping waves, the other hovering safely over land.

They're jammed. Not like fruit rolling boiled till the sugar charms the pectin, or my brother in the garage with amps and guitars. Jammed like fourteen lanes of the Santa Monica Freeway on any afternoon, miles of mechanized fires adding five degrees to the year-round summer.

They're spooning. Not like my mother doling out green beans. Spooning like we do in the night, falling asleep on opposite sides of the bed and waking to find that she's cornered me against the outside edge, snoring hot on my neck.

Canterbury Plains

I swagger, American farmboy I never was,
thick-trousered rustic pretense but joyful
in a chest-high canopy of Queen Anne's lace
or Queen Anne's snowflakes, maybe,
something fractal, like the ferns further upcountry,
infinite coil of curled up koru.

The wheat's a freeze frame of beige rain
quivering in the field, improbably vertical
terrestrial tassels strung up by invisible thread
stretched a hundred million miles to the
hydrogen gaslamp drifting overhead behind
a pilgrimage of chastely white clouds.

Highland cattle in shaggy summer misery
frame me in their trapezoidal horns, a trespasser
launching into Kiwi airspace a foreign missile:
a red white and scuffed cork-and-leather piece of home,
Rawlings baseball, falling in tight geometry
to the spanksound pocket of my glove.

The donkeys notice me, and look up quizzically,
grey uniformed generals awaiting bad news.
Ferdinand and Francesca leave their rusty tent,
their hairy, corrugated scratching post and
flick forward their ears, thick and steady as my forearm
and hot under my fingernails.

Southpaw sandwiched in cowhide, I walk back
clapping the ball with its smudges of donkey dust,
pitching it high in a sky where it doesn't belong
though it looks just the same: a fat little bird
darting for a darker blue, a grander view,
its underbelly in shadow.

Toilet Stop #4

Ammonia lockbox
crispy-still
flies in corners

Long-drop
Count the seconds
Plop

Nothing to flush
or wash – just zips
and buttons and

outside the sea air
the queue and
pass the paper on

Two bare bums
along the tree line
tired of waiting

laughing now
drowning ants
hot dirt fizzing

return to the van
so pleased with
their equipment

Boys on the Beach

Five hours in a gutless summer wonder like a Boys'
Brigade bus parading us north as we bitch
about the sticky-black leather back seat, treacle-thick heat
lazy fly fizzing, concussing on the glass, herds
of cattle startle, grazing in the grass, rheumy eyes see
us onward, heaving past banks draped daintily in

darker green, radiata pines with chewed up trim, interim
toothpick piles, onward, to gaptooth smiles from local boys
lollipop men in roadworks crews, onward, cruising out to sea
that salt-soup sloshing flat, washing in at Coopers Beach
where nighttime nudes, post-coitally subdued, can hear
the dogged ache of foreign waves collapsing without heed

for our clingfilm summer, humidity stew, my heartbeat pulsing heat
and I know it's this hair, Greek boy statue ring of curls, cool in
museum marble, maybe, but not in Greece and not here
in the flesh, dribbled sweat double-vision blur: bronze boys
in a sandstorm kaleidoscope, slick symmetry down the beach
on a brace of boogie boards, Styrofoam smack against the sea.

Floating palaces, moon-moored chariots for suntanned sultans, seen
here in foam-sewn ruffles like the leaders of the first gasping heat
of dusky demigods to reach us from some South American beach
where our Chilean doubles, Pacific palindromes, spoon, innocent
in the surf, wrapped tight like salty cocoons, then climb atop buoys
for a westward squint to the scouts they sent to find us out here

alone but twin-hearted already, underwater and yet able to hear
the plunging gurgles of the other. A single surge sets off the scene:
the Grecian boatman tumbles, sand-scraped, jumbled, just a boy-
child of crepe paper lungs, drugged by the heat
of the midday sun, dragged under, deadly thunder inundating
my ears until I'm grabbed up and lugged onto the beach

a bit limp at first, limbs slack, neck flaccid like the beached
baby hammerheads the fisherman sometimes find here
staring down Pōhutukawa pipecleaners dusting the shore, inert
with wide-eyed horror only two meters short of the breathable sea
that low-cut tidal tease, the ragged blue I now cough free, clumsy heat
tarting up my cheeks as I lean into the numbness of a boy

flecked with ocean grit and breathing still in squalls, beach
towel drawn around our skinnyboy shoulders, a hero
against the battering sea, he holds me to his chest, despite the heat.

When You Transition Without Me

I.

Your new friends
men who were never boys
are assholes.

Gender studies majors
turned teenage stereotypes
of try-hard masculinity

burping beers and
grabbing jam jars
from my hands.

Give it here, love.
Let a man have a go.

II.

We're not like this.
We wear blowaway cowlicks.
We read folktales at bedtime.
We pad over kelp to the sea.
We watch Māori television with subtitles.
We wear suits with buttonhole sprigs.

III.

I hate you around them.

Gruffing up your voice
walking elbows out
taking up all the space.

I'm embarrassed
watching you play
rugby-head for the lads

watching you put on
a grave masculine scowl

watching you give
girls the glad-eye.

And exhausted later
when you want reassurance
that you made a good man.

Winter Sun

In the afternoon, when the sun lights
the endless fall of dust particles, we
wonder if only we can see them

and keep wondering as we fell asleep,
your limbs wrapped around me,
a barnacle bigger than the boat,

and your fingers twitch
Morse code messages on my back
as you dream and then forget

you are dreaming, until you wake
and the room is grey and you
remember there is no color

without the light, except behind
my eyelids where my dreams
continue because I don't know

the sun has set and taken all the colors with it.

Save Radio New Zealand

When the radio deejay signs off
Good night, you glorious country
he means us, he means
high heels are a turn off,
keep your feet flat till he teaches
us to curl our toes.

He means for us to break hearts
in succulent glass gardens,
planetariums, post shops,
and the toilets at the rodeo,
nowhere so obvious as a
corner café called MASH.

He means for us to turn in now
dream of circus ladders, ourselves
at the top, turn ourselves in now
come whistling forward
when we realize we can't
stay balanced forever.

Picton's Morning Crust

The town wakes, rubbing its eyes of the curdled muck of infancy
once scooped free by mum's wet pinky.
The same mums now bounce behind predawn
zigzag dogs holding out for the perfect spot
though they've been holding it all night.

Schoolkids in fraying jumpers call to each other
over fences, stretching tall on the pedals of their fixies.
And hitchies just off the overnight ferry from
Wellington stake out tracts of motorway,
target demographics, road personas:

The globe-trotting hippie with his mountain man sack
and Medusa head of dusty coiled dreads.
Campervan patriarchs mutter and stare as he shrinks
in the rearview mirror, but the next load of stoners will stop
to see if he's got something to share.

The blonde in her pink parka heading south
to meet her man, an engineer digging out bodies
at the Pike River mine. But the truckies don't know that.
They'll pick her up for someone to talk to and she'll talk
nonstop about dead miners and her heroic boyfriend.

And me, with the dimpled face of a teenage runaway,
rugby league pillow under my arm, and a sign that says *Please*
still the magic word with mums everywhere:
the domesticated caffeine fiends who whistle
as they drop rubbish bags beside me on the curb,

the carpool drivers who toot twice and then lay on the horn,
the anxious mom who waits back in Michigan
for my Facebook status updates and someday return,
and the mum who must be coming soon
to scoop me up and out of Picton.

Another list of sorrows projected onto the landscape

Plastic bags slink and snap like cats.
Pak n' Save makes a yellow tom with no mate.

Braided rivers can never stay together.
They pick apart their slate grey beds.

Birds travel in pairs, even when one is dead.
The truck's horn ends the mourning early.

The cattle auctioneer always smells of shit.
Grown-up farm girls lie back and think of home.

Clouds break the backs of mountains, slowly.
The great rocks submit, like servicemen slumping in rest homes.

Sandflies are infinite.
You can't bargain with them, even for their lives.

Uretiti

Maybe I grew up here, maybe I got no older:
I can walk the length of this beach,
can run from campsite to industrial lights
like El Segundo where I once lost
Rosie's bikini bottom to the waves,

like Ravensbourne where we drove
the night I finally kissed Jo
three, four, five years ago
when I came to this country alone
with no sense of where I was going.

Now if I walk this beach again,
if I run with my eyes on the sky,
no matter how far I go, Orion stays still
getting no closer or farther away
like a photograph set before a treadmill.

But if I continue long enough into the night
at last, on his own, he seems to rise,
and the stars behind become bright
filling in the empty spaces until
all the shapes have changed.

Acknowledgments

First, thanks to Sven Davisson at Rebel Satori Press for championing the work of queer writers and shepherding this collection through publication during a pandemic.

The seeds of this collection can be found in the MFA thesis I completed at the University of Canterbury under the direction of John Newton, whose mentorship was invaluable. Michele Leggott was an incisive external reader of that early manuscript, as well as the first to record me reading my poems, which allowed me to approach them in a new way. I am grateful, too, to the broader New Zealand poetry community for nurturing my writing. In particular, thanks to Dave Eggleton at *Landfall*, Fergus Barrowman at *Sport*, and Paula Green at *NZ Poetry Shelf* for publishing and encouraging my work.

In revising this manuscript, I was surrounded by a fantastic group of Vermont writers. I offer huge gratitude to Penelope Cray, Maria Hummel, and Meg Reynolds, whose poetic instincts and eagle eyes greatly improved this collection. I also appreciate the insightful ideas and ongoing camaraderie of Ben Aleshire, Eve Alexandra, Elisabeth Blair, Duncan Campbell, Frances Cannon, Jari Chevalier, Kristin Fogdall, Didi Jackson, Major Jackson, Kerrin McCadden, Elizabeth Powell, Alison Prine, Tanya Stone, and Bill Stratton. Further thanks to Susanmarie Harrington and April Christenson for hosting the University of Vermont's faculty writing group.

To all those people, named and unnamed, who appear in this collection, transformed through poetic license, thank you for being part of my growing up. In particular, thank you to my parents, who got me through a difficult adolescence and encouraged my love of books from the time I was a tiny baby in a crib. And thank you to Emily Beam, who I love even more now than I did at sixteen – you lurk throughout this collection, and I couldn't have finished it without you.

Finally, I am grateful to the editors of the journals in which these poems first appeared:

Alluvium: Alternate Timeline, Apologetics of a College Freshman, Comfortable Grunge, Eight, Feed Me, Lone Pine Cemetery, The Strait, When you tire of your homeland
Borderlands: Texas Poetry Review: Field Trip
Carbon Culture Review: The Auto Pilot, Padiddle
Cream City Review: Sonoran Song
The Delmarva Review: The San Francisco Self-Examiner
Hawai'i Review: Boys on the Beach
Home is Where You Queer Your Heart (Foglifter Press): To San Francisco with Paul
JAAM: Boys on the Beach, The way it felt to be so warm
Landfall Review: Another List of Sorrows Projected onto the Landscape, Her Teeth, Otago, Picton's Morning Crust, Venice Beach
Nebo Literary Review: Toilet Stop #4
The New Zealand Listener: Shipwrecked, I Arrive
Outside In: They tell me I am wicked and I believe them
Red Savina Review: The only shame
Riprap Journal: The New Neighborhood
SATURNALIA '21 (Lupercalia Press): Her Blue Moons, The Man She Wants
Six Little Things: Shedd Aquarium
Spectrum Literary Journal: Peaches, Please don't hurt me, When You Transition Without Me

Spork: The Day Will Be Beautiful, Save Radio New Zealand
Sport: Uretiti, We Get On
Swimming with Elephants: Winter Sun
Turbine: Canterbury Plains, Telephones

CPSIA information can be obtained
at www.ICGtesting.com
Printed in the USA
BVHW071811211122
652433BV00002B/140

9 781608 642106